Real Bread

Poetry and Prose Inspired by the Famine of the Moment

LESA CALDARELLA-WONG

May 2016
To Doska,
Let is the Real
Bread of this life.
that thly nourishes
our soul.
Blessings always!
Lesa Caldarella-Wong

Hope has two beautiful daughters; their names are anger and courage. Anger at the way things are. Courage to make them the way they ought to be.
~ Saint Augustine

Real Bread

Poetry and Prose Inspired by the Famine of the Moment

LESA CALDARELLA-WONG

ISBN: 978-1939625-93-9
Library of Congress Control Number: 2014908468

Published by Inkwell Productions
10869 N. Scottsdale Road # 103-128
Scottsdale, AZ 85254-5280

Tel. 480-315-3781
E-mail info@inkwellproductions.com
Website www.inkwellproductions.com

Printed in the United States of America

Acknowledgements

I wish to recognize the following people whose words of encouragement and unique contributions I cherish, and who helped in bringing this work to fruition.

~ My husband, Wardon Wong, for his understanding and appreciation of my creative nature. For tolerating my crazy "writer's hours." For his patience and understanding about my need to write. We are truly the scientist and the poet; we are East meets West in the most wonderful way. I am grateful and know that without his love and support this book would have not been written.

~ Nikos Ligidakis, my writing mentor, for his passion for life, his guidance, his commitment, and for believing in me as a writer.

~ Inkwell Productions, my publisher, for their partnership. Special thanks to MaryEllen Smith, "editor extraordinaire," for smoothing over the rough spots and little imperfections while still maintaining the heart of the poetry. To Ron Birchenough, graphic artist, for his creativity and genius in design, and for patiently working with my photos some of which are more than twenty years old. For Barbara Heinemann's seamless behind-the-scenes work to bring this work to market and to promote it.

~ Sara Winston, for her patience, grace, and insight in reviewing each selection and offering suggestions that imparted clarity and spirit to the work.

~ Frederick Foote's command of the written word is a gift, and I am humbled that he took the time to review my book. His thoughtful critique and suggestions always resulted in improvement.

~ My fellow Sacramento writers Reginald Otto, Dominic Bulone, Jack Ratliff, Nicole Park, Doug Huse, Katie Quarles, and Tony Robles, whose support, immense talent, honesty, humor, and kindness gave me the impetus and vision to complete this work.

~ Karen Randau, for her guidance in helping me to traverse my journey as a writer. For the the many times she listened more than talked as I discussed matters of the soul and heart.

~ Sonja Starks, Marie Grandstaff, and Helene Gumina for being encouraging, transparent, and faithful friends for life. To Margaret Mungai, my Kenyon sister, for teaching me through her view of the world and service to others. To Margo Minor, my cousin and fellow poet, for inspiring me in ways she may never comprehend.

~ My sisters Lynda Caldarella, Cathee Rohr, Carla Narmore, Leslee Marcuri, and Cari Williams, who have urged me to publish my writing for years. You remain my first and constant confidants and biggest cheerleaders.

~ Finally, to my children Keith, Madonna, and Francesco, for being the muses in my shadows and for holding up a mirror to my soul and bringing joy and purpose to my life.

EXTRAORDINARY PRAISE FOR

Real Bread

Diving into these words was an exercise in bearing witness to a part of the human experience I had only read about in the newspapers. I remember reading about Rwanda. I prayed. But I was removed. Reading *Real Bread* was a journey into the darkest parts of humanity; haunting and harrowing, yes, but bearable and illuminating because Lesa Caldarella-Wong bore witness with love, with the eyes and heart of God as embodied within as a "woman from the West."

These poems are potent and relevant reminders for all of us today, twenty years later, of the suffering that still exists around the world...and the loving actions of the extraordinary ordinary people acting to bring light and love in the form of medicine, bread, water, kindness.

I am impressed by the eloquence of the language, the depth of connection, and how Ms. Caldarella-Wong was able to convey the unbearable with such grace and dignity and respect for the country and its people.

~ **Sheila James**, Mediator and Collaborative Attorney

Poet-Author Lesa Caldarella-Wong offers in *Real Bread: Poetry and Prose Inspired by the Famine of the Moment,* a profound "pageantry and truth/served in the finest cups." Her thinking "lives in a moment of being," where pageantry and truth survive in "a place where children are fragile birds." In Ethiopia, "without pretense to adorn my fears," she writes of crushing poverty that pierces deep into her soul, to the homage of spirit catching tears, and presents us with the grateful and sincere "last remnants of civility."

~ **Gordon Preston**, Author, *Pieces of Monterey Bay*

Lesa Caldarella-Wong feels intensely, and that is at the core of her gift. It is a gift that gives her the ability to use her feelings and words to paint indelible pictures for the reader. It is her journey, and it becomes our journey, too.

In the poem *Sparrow Child,* the words are so raw, sparse, and real that they left my mouth agape. In *Glow on the Hill,* I can feel the wrenching passion of a mother's experience at King Faisal Hospital. And in the beautiful *Acacia*, one can't help but feel a somber peace for scores of people who live on in hope.

This is an amazing first book of poetry and prose. It is definitely one that you will want to share with friends.

~ **Marguerite Minor**, Poet-Author

Caldarella-Wong's keen insight into hearts of the babies, children, teens, and adults she witnesses first-hand is breathtaking; she is an extraordinary storyteller who uses masterfully selected and poetic words to help us feel empathically for these desperate and very proud souls.

Her gift is in never stripping anyone she observes of their dignity—always holding them in the highest. Caldarella-Wong's powerful words take the reader to the same places that touched her soul. Without preaching, she writes in such a way that I feel her heart.

I've known Lesa since we were in junior high and joined an after-school Chinese class. Even then her curiosity about people who live in cultures much more diverse than our almost 100-percent Caucasian, small–Southern California town burned passionately. Taking the curiosity and compassion I know she has for people in all corners of the globe and turning it into the art of lovely poetry makes the words take on an elegance that contrasts with the difficult things she describes.

~ **Sue Breding**, Award-Winning Journalist

Caldarella-Wong's songs of experience are at once a blend of immeasurable passion, frightful imagery, and unending hope. Her words are a beacon to those who would sacrifice for the betterment of our planet, and the strength and purpose of her message will tingle the very fiber of your soul. Bravo!

~ **Kevin Connard**, Teacher and Author, *Hollymac*

"The wealth of a soul is measured by how much it can feel; its poverty by how little."

~ William Alger

Real Bread

Foreword

In *Real Bread,* Lesa Caldarella-Wong has strung together a necklace of hideous, brutal stones: indifference, ignorance, racism, genocide, violence, famine, starvation, greed, fear, and the lust for power. She has polished these bitter rocks with amazing images and gut-wrenching emotions. She has cut and set these stones in modern times in ancient settings in Ethiopia, Rwanda, Mozambique, and Kenya, as well as at home in the United States. In the facets of these morally blinding, brilliant gems we see ourselves reflected in an unhealthy and unholy light.

In and among these monstrous stones are pearls of faith, grace, love, and caring. We wear this necklace as a noose or a necktie; either way, it grows uncomfortably tight. I believe the hope of this book is that we will look and see and feel the world we are making.

If you eat this *Real Bread,* it will bruise your throat and stir your soul. It is a powerful, wonderful collection of vivid realities made personal, painful, aand unforgettable. Thank you to Ms. Caldarella-Wong for being there and for writing this.

~ **Frederick Foote,** Author, Attorney and Retired College Professor

A little bit of my heart was broken; a part of me will be changed forever. This collection is essential reading, more than ever, in a time where there is so much conflict in so many places, and yet many of us are cozily tucked away. Stunning, visual, authentic, brutal, and so very human, this book will drag you out of your comfortable complacency and force you to connect with the realities of your world.

Utterly engaged, I did not want to stop reading. This felt like an important book. It is essential that the images of *Real Bread* are shared with us the naïve reader, lest we forget the impact that we may have. This is not someone else's world; this is our world. This book, and these journeys made by another, is a powerful immersion into the author's raw exposure to all that our world may be.

The poetry is often devastating, dragging you into the depth of evil that humanity can execute and the fragility of life. At other moments, this poetry touches the heart with fragments of light and moments of hope. It is, put simply, a staggering book about all corners of humanity that will touch your heart and leave you altered.

My comments are not idle flattery. It is a powerful piece of writing which made me cry and I found myself both with so many words, so many adjectives…but at the same time, wordless.

~ **Emma Hazeldine,** Postgraduate Researcher, Plymouth University, EN

Table of Contents

III. Losing Sleep

IV. Pale Dogs

Dedication

In loving memory of my parents,
who saw my path long before I took the first
step – and who nurtured the poet and artist within

To Wardon – I am forever grateful.
I waited all my life …
Darling, you are "my Charlie"

To the sparrow child, the common fish, and the
pale dog for teaching me to find treasure
in the famine of the moment

I

Treasures of Aksum

*It is a curious phenomena that God has made the hearts of
the poor, rich and those of the rich, poor.*

~Vinoba Bhave

jabena

entering Bahir Dar
on the shores of Lake Tana
cradling gracious the Nile Blue
papyrus Tankwa carry the fisherman's
treasure and trade

great waterfalls tell stories of the ancients –
revealing secrets of cardamom and bent reed
of Weyto and obelisks
castles of Gondor – churches of Lalibela

whispering legends of emperors and Aksum kingdoms
the mothers and daughters of Sheba
offer ceremony
roasting coffee and grinding spice

jabena brewed and sugared
pageantry and truth
served in the finest cups

scattering scarlet petals upon the earth
a simple gesture in the curve of the day

Bees

It is still.

I am surrounded.
They are swarming like bees
in a spherical motion.

Waiting in the noonday sun.
Neither sheltered or
protected from the angry drought.

Dressed in Bible story garments,
draped and flaccid melting rags

Hiding babies
beneath fraying burlap capes.
Mute and staring,

Pointing at me. A spectacle of the West,

I am penetrated by their pain,
assaulted by the void in this moment.

I feel the twists of their empty stomachs,
The growls of fading beasts living within their bodies.

Hills surround the barren parched land.
The only sound is the whistling of the wind
magnifying the silence and the stares.

Mouths open
showing me their crosses.
Empty plastic NGO issue bowls at their feet,
Anticipating manna.

They are like bees
without buzz.

Without blossom.
Without honey.

Scrolls

I am bereft of worldview,
A voyeur of suffering and poverty
reflecting on this pause in my journey,
sitting silent,
savoring this meal,
sumptuous fare
for the communion of this moment.
White toast with marmalade,
Hard-boiled eggs,
Sugared Ethiopian coffee,
Strong and mud-thick.

The day unfolds like a papyrus scroll
with stories of hidden blossoms
among the sparrow child and pale dogs

Nestled in the growls of empty stomachs
and the fragrance of roasted cardamom and pestled spice

Tradition and history inhabit this land,
offering refuge to sacred relics
and sanctuary for Dinknesh.

I am humbled knowing I have walked on this holy ground
thinking my loaves and fishes would feed the starving,
that my God would save their souls.

Not every tale is of brokenness and famine
cradling the origins of the angels.

Wholeness is at the essence of this world
evident in the child shepherd
wandering the barren hills, staff in hand,
herding his goats and sheep.

A child of eight wearing threadbare rags for clothes,
an orthodox cross around his neck.

No matter the lack of possessions and food,
his determination rises.

He is complete in his joy;
he is without sin.

The spirit runs deep through
the Nile Blue.

I have been fed.
I have been saved.

Sparrow Child

"Where are the children, the tiny ones?"
"There are supposed to be children?"

Woman with emblazoned blue crown across her forehead
speaking, mouthing low whispers,
A cackle, a hum, undistinguishable words.

Vomitus-tortured glance.
Leathered, golden,
hunger-worn, angular-framed face

Opens her dervish's cape
revealing a fragile bird of a child
hanging hopeless on her desiccated breast,

Orange-red down for hair,
a sparrow suckling without cry.

Protruding belly.
Empty hollow of a child.

Skin dangling like wet silk
on a humid day.

Old man face
on the body of a small child.

Impression and presence so thin and slight.
There is no noticeable sparkle in the baby's eyes,
just sagging skin and a fowl-like spine.

Empty Bowls

The land is desolate and bleak
Clouds have deserted the skies

Thirsty for rain, the hills are all dry
Rolling on like an ocean
Of empty waves

No end to the tide of lack
Meadows are bristled like straw
Without blossom or blade

The wind blows hot and sharp
Cutting angry swaths in barren terrain

Vacant remembrance of what used to be
Leaving nothing but shadows and prayers
Destroying the cattle and grain

Silencing the rattle of empty bowls
Drowning the precious in anguish and dust

Moment

This moment and place
It is not about you or me

This vocation of service and becoming
is a flowing river

A way for God's love and grace
to touch faces and hearts

It is our moment of being –

When we can go to the hidden places
where creation hides and weeps

The moment for us to harmonize with
the melody of the Beloved

To be the zephyr and shroud
to wrap the lost and searching in

To gently wake the sleepy
and heal the errant creatures

It is the moment to spite our own sin
We become and we live

It is not about our lives
or our interpretation of the spirit

We cannot have all the answers

We can only be the music
and the banks of the river
And hope to be the satin ribbon
blowing in the wind

Giving peace and beauty as a gift
Bidden with grace and gifted mystery

It is not about you and not about me
We are only a part of a piece of God's dream

It is about the whole creation
and sacred destiny

It is about the universal song
where everything belongs

Wella Balsam

It has been three weeks since I washed my hair. Wearing a hat every day. Sweat dripping from my forehead – extreme hat-hair. Dressed in a cross between safari and missionary garb. Thrift-store khaki head to toe. My conservative skirt outdated and too long. Covering, but not hiding, my femininity. Socks and sandals.

I count the weeks in *Time* magazine covers
May 9 Nelson Mandela
May 16 "There are no devils left in Hell," the missionary said.
"They are all in Rwanda."
May 23 Cosmic Crash
May 30 Jacqueline Bouvier Kennedy Onassis, 1929–1994

"Jambo Mademoiselle, welcome to the Nairobi InterContinental."

Stately and well-appointed modern hotel. The staff is attentive with the pomp and circumstance of colonial influence and the depth of Kenyan warmth. Four stars. Beautiful marble pillars grace the lobby. Lines form at the registration desk.

I will stay two days – send my clothes to laundry. Write postcards to family and friends – send words of optimism. Offer my reflections on world peace and ending hunger. Compile trip notes. Go to the hotel hair salon.

While I am here the children still suffer. There is nothing I can give or do that will help. I am without excuses and reason. My hands are open, my baskets are empty.

Famine in Ethiopia, landmines in Mozambique, widespread HIV in Uganda.
Somalia has just thrown out all NGOs, and the situation in Rwanda is getting worse every day.
The bodies thrown in the Akagera are now on the shores of Lake Victoria, dissolving into the soil, glistening as they recede, creating holy ground.

The absurdity and profundity of this moment is beyond my abilities and resource.
I hole myself up in my hotel room.
Hopefully I will sleep.

The room is clean. Modern. Beautiful western décor. Television.
I remove my hat and sandals,
gather laundry.

David the steward knocking at the door. "Jambo, please Madame, may I be so kind to help you?" I hand him a pile of laundry and my hat.

"Yes, yes, Madame, the laundry will be ready tomorrow. Do you want starch, Madame?"
I smile and nod.
I order baguette, butter, and wine from room service.
I have a hot bath.

CNN buzzing in the background. Static companion. The advertisement for The Carnivore and Treetops Lodge repeat every fifteen minutes.

The wine is warm and awful.

I am tired. I hold my rosary without whispering the prayers, trying to find God in between the magazine covers and hair washings.

I sleep under clean sheets with the television rattling in the background, trying to drown out my thoughts.

I have a nightmare.
The dream repeats over and over like the commercial for the Treetops Lodge.
Famine in Ethiopia. Landmines in Mozambique. I am drinking tea. There are refugees running into Uganda from Rwanda. Tutsi running for their lives. Something terrible is happening. Hutu in Goma. There is no food, no clean water. Cholera outbreaks. The river is red. Bodies in the river, bodies floating in Lake Victoria. Something terrible is happening.

Morning; room service.

Tea, toast, marmalade, paw-paw with lime.

The Daily Nation headline – "Turmoil in Rwanda Continues"

I write cards to family and friends.

I sip my tea.

The television drones on.

I hold my rosary. I cannot whisper the prayers.

I fall asleep and wake up to David knocking at the door, "Jambo, please Madame, your laundry," he says with a big smile.

He hands me the folded and nicely starched blouses and pants. All my socks and underwear are wrapped in paper and neatly arranged in a basket. My hat is on the top of the pile.

He looks at me embarrassed and picks up the hat. "Oh, I am so sorry, Madame, your hat is small."

It now looks like a child's hat, shrunken from the hot water washing. I hold back my laughter. A bright funny spot in my day. I smile. "Asante sana, David."

CNN reports about Rwanda. The situation is escalating while the world looks away.

I call my parents. Crying, I tell them, "It is awful and there is nothing we can do. The UN can't even help them."

She tries to comfort me, not understanding the world I have chosen to live in.

I stop crying.
I share the story about the laundry,
the hat, and the warm wine.
We laugh.

I picture my Italian mother sitting in her kitchen with her cold cup of coffee.
She has lit a candle for me. She is holding back her tears.
She promises to whisper prayers for me on her rosary.
To pray for the children.
We say goodbye and I love you.

I will check out of the hotel in less than twenty-four hours.

It is three p.m.

I call the hotel hair salon. They are not busy; my appointment is at three-thirty.

Arriving.
"Jambo, madame."

The smell of Wella Balsam permeates the room.

Unfolding Rainbows

Package full of prisms
bursting ripe with splendor

Violet crimson crowns

Empty clouds of quiver
their fullness tumbling down

Heavens dropping rain
washing rocks and trees

Adding gloss and shimmer
without a cry or sound

Painting roads with honey
kissing clean the leaves

Waters dancing aimless
Streams their saunter flows

Marching through the madness
down mountains, waltzing free

Catching fears and hopes
answering maiden's plea

Courting amble showers
in the torrent of the gale

Tumbling rocks to gems
as splendor does unfurl

Sands turn into diamonds
gracing dawn with pearls

Unlocking bursts of sunshine
with their passionate embrace

Raindrops full of fury
blessing green the scape

Artist of the thunder –
hear the warriors' cry

As they paint the visage
of the flower's golden blush

Skies now tinted amber
in the veracity of deep

Reserving our salvation
throughout the senseless storm

Until the sadness ceases
in the shadows of the rush

Transporting pain and sorrow
the tempest now asleep

Radiant moment waiting
with luminous colors glow

Sacred gifts before us
unfolding rainbow's brilliance
with the healing of our soul

gaze

our voices still
the darkness cold –

the night sky is folded out
like diamonds upon velvet

the only sound
our heartbeat echoing in the dark

millions of cerulean silver stars
dance across the Ethiopian heavens
holding the spiky points of their hands

forming a circle around the world
in line with the equator
like a long piece of silver lace

planets appear without explanation
the moon captivates our moments

morning is tucked away
with the sun behind the horizon
a golden sweet fruit
from the basket of Sheba
hiding in the pocket of the ocean

we are without the threads
of our truth until dawn
until then we will gaze
at the sky above Aksum
waiting to unlock the secrets of day

White Rivers
Addis Ababa, 1994

From my
hotel window
Crisp morning

Cockerel's crow
coaxing Sun
From Dawn's pocket
Illuminating
clouds with silver

Adhan beckons devotees
from the highest minaret
Echoing sacred chants
on faded cracked colonial facades

Roads damp with the honey glaze
of Midnight rain –
Tires hiss and spit
through the commuter rush

Songs of doves
slowly fading as
the honking of Lada Taxis
fill the air

Orthodox priest
in full regalia

leading procession
with silver cross
parting seas and sidewalks

Men in long white shirts
and prayer shawls
trimmed in gold threads
walk behind, carrying icons

Women with white natella head-
coverings follow –
matching tempo in every step
Creating a cadence of
mantra and prayer

Over packed mule carts crowd
shoppers in the narrow
walkways to the Merkato

Market stalls and
lean-to shacks with
corrugated metal roofs
share horizon and curb
Their hands open
with fingers touching
walls old and new

Cradling ancient churches
and pristine hotels –

Blight and progress intertwines
the world of the Nile Blue

Diesel fuel, burning trash,
and roasting coffee rises –
blossoming full
perfuming the city
in the morning heat

Disciples flood the streets
in pallid vestments
paving the well-worn paths
forming a great
white river of impenetrable
history and strength

Addis is swirling with
the beauty and reverence
of the veils and rosaries of
many religions and cultures

Holding promise and pearls
within her palms –
Swaddling beggar and banker
in the hope and poverty of the city

Reminding Me

Staff in hand
Joy apparent
Herding the goats in

Boy in Bible clothes
Gauze-like
Burlap fashion statement
Faded prince's garment
Hanging from his bony frame

Happiness
Overflowing his countenance
Knowing his Father owns
The cattle on a thousand hills

Possessing grace
Standing regal
Mustering the dignity and strength
Of a soldier of the plains

To spite his lack
A shepherd of the kingdom
On this holy ground

Reminding me
Our souls and dreams
Are all the same

in need of lovers

the grapes not yet ripe for harvest
we drink the wine from yesterday
until our laughter rolls with the hills
forming waves beyond the horizon
caught in the silk of the day

making us forget the tragic moments
the wasted blush and devotion

surrendering our verse upon the grasses
swaying like dancers
so close there are no footsteps
bending the wrinkles of the wind

waiting for
the silver veil, the primordial moon to return
to answer the prayers within her pocket

for the honey to coat the mornings with radiance
bringing warmth to the bones of branch and bud

as we bow to ancient altars
with unspoken refrain
the breezes cast their spells
on the blossoms glowing gold

leaving the vines full to the bough
yielding gracious open virgins
the sweet and ripe sacrifice

with fruit presenting effortlessly
like scarves unfurling graceful on the bed

resting soft and sacred on the altar
naked and in need of lovers

II

Land
of a Thousand Hills

Everything in life is speaking in spite of its apparent silence.
~ Hazrat Inayat Khan

> *For all the animals of the forest are mine,*
> *and I own the cattle on a thousand hills*
> Psalms 50:10

A Thousand Hills

le pays des mille collines

Walking in the village among the pale dogs
Without pretense to adorn my fear
Feeling the cold hard clay
Caress the sandals on my feet

Entering the palaces of merchants and kings
Peddling their products and wares

Breathing in the clouds of dust
Parading the leaps and jumps of children
Who run among the market maze
With swollen bellies and matted rusted hair

Weaving through the crowd
Casting their mischievous stares –
Without a worry – unaware of their poverty

Void of the trappings of civilized fare
A stark simplicity

Their wealth outshining their fate
Like the richness of silk and thick cream

When you compare
The thousand hills within their command
The gifts I thought to bring
Are out shadowed and worthless

I am only a passing sojourner –
Disappearing in the dust
Invisible but for my obvious dismay

Astounded by their profundities
The famine of the moment
Is deep within my soul

Glow on the Hill

Rwanda – the land of a thousand hills – beautiful country. Inviting. Lush. Green. The Switzerland of Africa.

The sun is setting and everything has a grey silhouette. The outlines of banana trees and the profiles of hills are visible in the fading dusk.

The night greets us –
Balmy.
Peaceful and warm breezes.

Bombed and vacant buildings – altars of rubble – pay homage to the dead. Carcasses of burnt cars litter the side of the road.

We pass the peacekeepers on patrol, neutered of the ability to defend. We drive on; a curious fear occupies the air.

The sky is opaque; the indigo darkness transfuses the ether. The moonlight barely bleeding through illuminates the people walking on the road.

Without shoes, their clothes in tatters, threadbare and filthy, crusted with mud and the DNA of terror.

The ghosts and children walk hand in hand. Some have gashes and fresh wounds.

There are no fathers to protect them, or mothers to catch their tears. There are no old people to tell them the stories of the past.

They are flightless fowl carrying the last remnants of civility in the bedrolls and baskets teetering on their heads.

Our driver circles the wrong way through the roundabout, just missing a pickup truck filled with gun-toting child-soldiers. We all scream. They are anxious warriors. Beautiful young boys holding their guns erect and careless.

There is no power, no running water, no marketplace. Very little food. There are no hotel rooms.

The only lights are from King Faisal Hospital on the hill.

Following the glow, we find a sliver of humanity in the aftermath of the bloodletting. The hospital is a refuge of hope and healing for those beaten with clubs and slashed with panga.

Two doctors from the West – young, newly christened by the devastation of the holocaust.

Doing amputations without anesthesia. Have not slept for days.

Pensive. Disheveled. Exhausted.

There is very little suture material. Piecing together injuries with tightly wrapped bandages, covering the multitude of sins and wounds.

They give us a tour.

The OR – a smear of red on stainless steel. Needles soaking in Betadine. Scissors, scalpels, piles of gauze. Aspirin.

The recovery ward – two to a bed. No sheets, few blankets. Makeshift IV hung from the broken drapery rod.

Children huddled together for warmth. They manage smiles and laughter, peeking from behind their bandages.

Some are missing arms and legs; some bloody and dirty; some dying. All of them injured. Deep wounds. Damaged.

Yellow sticky note – ICU. Small naked boy around eight or nine years old. His eyes blackened and tightly shut – beaten. His face and skull so swollen, he looks like a hydrocephalic child.

He is trembling, curled in a fetal position. Trauma-induced autism.

Saw his family slaughtered. Was left for dead. Hid in the bush for three days.

I touch his hand and he flinches, moaning. His body recedes into a tight ball.

This child needs his mother to hold him. He is alone. I want to crawl up beside him and comfort him.

I want to stroke his brow and whisper,
"Mommy is here – it's OK."

The doctors both have tears in their eyes. They tell me this child is dying.

There are no words between us.

There are reports of continued attacks and landmines. It is beyond human comprehension.

We share tea with the doctors and stay the night at King Faisal Hospital. We sleep on old gurneys in an abandoned surgery room.

The sound of the wind and howling dogs scavenging on human carrion at the edge of city is in the distance.

The images of dying children without their mothers will forever haunt me.

Peacekeepers

War and poverty are the foreplay of this tragedy.
Peacekeepers pacing the streets outside the UNAMIR complex
Insuring security and "peace."

Armed and unable to defend,
Wearing flak jackets through the countryside,
Shooting the pale dogs scavenging in the streets.

Curious term, "Peacekeeper."
The damage has already been done;
Panga has sliced through everyone's souls.

still there

every day when we drive up the hill
the same death smell precedes –
the nauseous sight

the carcass of a pale dog rotting in the sun,
melting like a candle into the pavement.

after five weeks it is still there
the form of the animal is
barely recognizable,

the smell of death lingers.

we are there to find the children
those left in the bush –
victims of the slaughter.

we see them next to a hill
glistening in the daylight,
spirits hovering above.

landmines keep us away.

there is no one to bury the children,
no one to move dead animals

the smell of death is still there

Imana

Where is the savior of this tragedy?
The Balm of Gilead to heal these wounds?
The cup of cold water to quench our thirst?
"Imana yirirwa ahandi igataha mu Rwanda."
"God spends the day elsewhere, but sleeps in Rwanda."
There is no need to pray. Imana knows.

No Heroes

Newly appointed soldiers,
nine, ten … fourteen, fifteen years old,
piling into the back of pickup trucks
armed with assault rifles, drunk with
fear and power.
Their only dignity exists in the uniforms they wear,
camouflaging their anguish and grief.

I have pity for them,
knowing they heard the cry of the innocent silenced in mid-scream
and have watched their mothers and sisters beaten and raped,
tossed into the bush like rubbish and left for dead.

They have seen the souls ripped from babies with panga
and the spines of virgins severed before orgasm.

There is no cure to heal their pain.

We kid ourselves to think that we really have something
to offer the Child Warriors –

No longer free to play,
they traverse carefully through fields
to avoid the trip wires and landmines,
watching as friends lose limb and spirit.

I hear laughter, and for a moment they almost seem normal,
like my own son

Waving arms and pointing guns at the sky.
As the truck pulls away it is silent
but for the sound of birds and the tires driving through mud.

They stare through us, cutting molecules
Void of sparkle and light.
What it is in their eyes?
It is not joy.
It is not tears.

There is still blood seeping from this tragedy.
They are soon to be forgotten children.
There are no heroes.

Closed Eyes

If I don't scream, is there no pain?

If I don't fight, what will remain
of this sweetness and this truth in me?
Of the horror of darkness of dreaded dreams?

I will close my eyes and think
of distant lives,

When I was pure
and I was free,
and not burdened
with their evilness –

When I just gave
and served my God.

But I am here,
in awe
of just how evil
these demons are

That they could take the
essence of
the goodness inside me

Without concern for what becomes
of the blood and the soul
breaking that which makes me whole,

Entering where angels only tread,
shattering my preciousness

I close my eyes
without tears,
I swallow hard beneath my fear.
I keep within that part of me
that cloaked and tiny sanity.

I will rise when devils fall
and overcome their cruelty,
transforming stones to radiant jewels
to restore my treasured sanctity.

Bubble Wrap

Damn! We are out of bottled water.

There is no marketplace, no stores. The city is emptied of commerce. I ask a soldier from Senegal for some water. "No water to drink – no running water ... "Madame, it is not safe to drink the water." "Non-potable, madame, non-potable ..."

Razor wire surrounds this bombed out hotel, the UNAMIR fortress. A complete city within these ruins; generators, fax machines, computers, and hot coffee.

We have charmed the major for a place to sleep for the night, giving graceful our smiles and telling jokes.

There is no communion, no red wine for this Italian-Catholic girl. I am drinking vodka and warm beer with the comrades and peacekeepers ...

They issue us jerrycans to flush the toilet and bubble wrap to sleep on. There are three of us. We are tired. I don't care where we sleep, as long I don't have to give my pearls to the soldiers.

The peacekeepers are pacing the street in front of the compound. RPF soldiers in trucks cruise the roads. The city is dark. Only the UN headquarters and King Faisal Hospital have generators for light. The moonlight is piercing through the shattered building.

We are still, humbled and quiet. We say nothing and robotically prepare for sleep. We lay the bubble wrap down and use our packs as pillows.

Without discussion, we line up in unison, side to side, lying on the floor, spoon to spoon. Awkward source of warmth and comfort in the dampness and fear lingering in the night.

Sleeping without cover, fully clothed with my hiking boots laced – knife, flashlight, and rosary at hand.

I cover my ears to block out the distant sounds of mortar.
The pale dogs howling through the night create a haunting white sound. An eerie soundtrack – the evil progeny of the bloodbath.

I fall asleep and dream.

I am crying, quoting the Bible to my mother. "I just want to save the widows and the fatherless." I walk outside and pet the goat next to the fence. Then I am in my bed at home and I can feel the sheets against my skin, cool and soft. In the next scene I am in a field of flowers and I am dancing. I see a woman in Rwandan-style clothing with a small boy. The boy has a machete wound on his head. They invite me into a small room – a tiny home. They offer me tea and biscuits. The tea is hot and sweet; the biscuit tastes awful and I throw it on the floor. The woman said it was sprayed with insecticide. I am back in the field but a soldier tells me I can't pick the flowers because there are landmines. I try to find the path back to the road. I walk to an abandoned building, and once inside I am trapped and can't move because there are trip wires. In the next scene I am by the fence and a boy with a machete is smiling at me next to the goat. He looks up at me and then cuts the goat's throat. I gasp. I pick the flowers by the fence and throw them and walk away.

I wake up to the sound of gunshots when I roll over.

It is the bubble wrap popping.

Now fully awake, I prop myself against the wall of the vacant room, looking at the moonlight peering through the bullet holes and waiting until the sun rises.

Silage

A thousand hills erupt
teeming with sorrow and despair
turning the Akagera red and blue

Filling the potholes and open sewers
with the molten blood of children
bubbling up from the volcano

Rotting vaporous in the streets
without name or number

Left as ash and refuse at the edge of town –
silage for the rats and pale dogs.

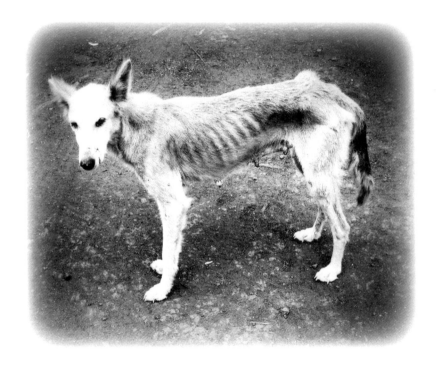

Potter's Field

Hutu killing Tutsi.
Tutsi pretending to be Hutu to save their lives.

Friends killing friends
with panga and primitive clubs.

Unborn babies ripped from their mother's bellies,
crushed and mangled.

Children slaughtered in the bush.

Women raped with knife and sticks,
eviscerated and splayed,

Stripped of dignity and song.

People left for dead in the streets –
tossed like garbage into mass graves.

The devils spare no one.

The Akagera is a floating grave,
thousands of bodies washing up on the shores
and islands of Lake Victoria.

Innocents –
missing limbs and faces.

Without names,
disintegrating into the lake's generous womb
creating a riparian potter's field.

Howling

In the day the pale dogs
run beside the barefoot children
kicking up billows of dust.

They never bark or growl;
they cower and scatter –

Frightened of the merchant's shout
and fearful of the marketplace clatter.

They are frail and skittish,

Faithful friend to the angels
with swollen bellies

Hoping to get a crust of bread
that drops upon the ground.

In the darkness, under the reflection of the moon
The dogs howl and show their angry teeth

Searching for food in the dump
at the edge of the city.

Dragging the dead from the heap
they are vicious and eat with abandon,

Howling in the dark
in harmony with
the souls hovering above

Until the sun arrives and the dogs
return to the children,

Docile and weak,
humble creatures

Waiting for crumbs and sup,
walking among angels and dust.

Shroud of Turin

Dirt road. Landmines. Two jeeps – one set of tire tracks.

Intentional slow pace. Quiet. No people.

Bringing emergency supplies and medicines.

Arriving, children singing, playing.
Speaking the language of laughter.

Deliberate happiness. Smiles. Some children are deaf – some blind – all injured. Offering greetings.

Hiding machete wounds under hats that look like toilet seat covers. One child tips his colorful toilet seat cover hat, bowing.

"Bonjour Mademoiselle, bonjour Monsieur," he says, bowing in respect.

He smiles and runs off to play with his buddies.

The Belgian priest tells us this is a special school for deaf and blind children. He has just arrived to help. There are no other adults alive.

He tells us this story.

"During the slaughter, all the adults were killed or ran away.

Many children were murdered or left for dead.

For days the deaf walked in trances,
The blind stumbled among their dead friends.

The deaf could not hear the tortured cries; the mute had no voice
to scream.

The blind had no vision of the horrible sight, but could hear
everything – feeling the splattering of blood on their faces.

The children, frightened and injured, fled to the bush. Hiding.
Terrified. They had no food or water. They ate leaves to survive.

Finally they returned – they groped in the darkness, trying to
locate the dead.

I found them dragging the bodies and bones of their dead
playmates from the courtyard and buildings wanting to bury
them – trying to dig shallow graves with their bare hands."

He brings us to the graveyard.

There are a few straggled flowers and primitive crosses placed
to honor the dead.

Stepping gingerly around the graves
in awe of the spirits that surround us –

Those of the dead
and those of the determined children
who survived and witnessed
the atrocities.

Walking through the courtyard,
the buildings are reduced to dust and rubble –
Evidence of mortar attacks.

In perfect form, gracing the holy ground –
A "Turin Shroud" outline remains of the imprinted stains of
children's bloody shadows on the stone paving.

Acacia

Blessing this holy ground
as you departed the manor,

Hiding your spirit
in the canopy of the trees
nestled into the sacred blossoms,

You have left only the petals on the path
Gifting the breezes in the night,
allowing the fragrance to waft through
veils of sadness with the elegance of cream.

Although you no longer tread the garden path,
we will never betray the legacy that you leave,

Your memory resting peacefully
in the music of our dreams,
the acacia holding mysteries
vast and deep
like doves upon the branch
nesting in the curve of our sleep.

We miss your laughter and your strength.
We are reminded in our sorrow that
we have only to gaze out the windows
and take in the green,

Pausing in the grace of the moment
between the hope and the rush,
We treasure your sacred song,
pervasive and enduring,

Bringing comfort to our grief,
gifting us the fragrance of flowers
and the lushness of trees.

Hawaii

The fields abundant
with silent treasure

Green and graceful sway,
lush with bananas decorating trees

Breezes like cream, wrapping round the fruit
light shining misty through the clouds,
the fog haunting and delicate
a gauze without salve.

The air is sweet with the shadow of
angels hovering above the bounty.

Beauty surrounds
this sacred domain of the precious
and the weak,

Blossoms gracing sorrow
without reason or explanation,

Child and creature among the carpets of gold,
forgotten in this garden of dreams,

Arusha abandoned.

The water drains both ways –
spiraling down, blue and red,
painting mud and dust with
the devil's play,

Graveyard in the heat of the equator
adding fire to the carnage bursting
ripe with Eden's fate.

If we look close enough we can see
the souls of children exploding in the horizon.

There are no sanctuaries,
no churches to shelter the poor,

No playgrounds or baskets
to gather new fruit.

The crops will all stay
untouched, unpicked
and uneaten

With humbled and fearful paces
creeping past the roundabout, dodging roadblocks
and slaughter,

The farmers are walking away
with their existence
and hope balanced on their heads.

The children follow like quails
behind the mother bird.

They only take what can be carried
in their palms.

The jewels have all scattered among the ashes and
blood.

Walking like lemmings in search of a cliff
so they can fall
into another life –

Dreaming of Hawaii.

Canopy

Looking at the trees from this space
That is truly all that exists

Absolute and perfect
Void of suffering and tears

Their happiness in the nape of the branch
Their leaves conscious and welcoming

Unaware of their beauty

As if the flower and branch and bud were always there
And the trees in their wholeness just appeared
In a stroke of satisfaction and magic

As if we were sent an angel to tells us
The joy is here
The banquet has been set
And we can have our fill

That as sure as the pearls are in our hands
The treasure exists in this moment

There are no seasons –
No shedding of leaves
Or blooming of flowers

No pain
No laughter

Only the trees
Standing without intent
Grateful to be giving shade

Gracing the moment complete
Their canopy outstretched and receiving

No Bread or Fishes

The world looks past the thousand hills
the aftermath of Mogadishu

ignoring the fatherless
disregarding the widows

deafening our ears to their cries
blinding our sight from the tragedy –

void of succor and tears
our hands remain closed

offering no cups of cold water
no bread or fishes

Borrowing

With sweetness running from my chocolates
I borrow honey from the morrow

Knowing that my strength is not just defined
in this moment but in my ability
to grasp the nectar of the light before the stars appear

Crawling meek and silent,
carefully adding stones
and candles to my low-lying altar

Taking with me and holding to heart
the secrets that will heal this brokenness
and shroud my curve among the angel's shadow

So that to spite my fragility and flaws,
my inability to carry all
the pearls within the palms of my hands

I am borrowing baskets from
the moments that do not yet exist

To carry the last bits of chocolate and sweetness
to the high places upon the land

Capturing all the jewels from this altar,
borrowing valor and grace

Living peaceful in this moment

I seek eternity,
taking loan from tomorrow
and reclaiming my strength

"The love of a single heart can make a world of difference.
I believe that we can heal Rwanda –
and our world – by healing one heart at time."
~ Immaculee Ilibagiza

III
Losing Sleep

We must never permit the voice of humanity within us to be silenced. It is man's sympathy with all creatures that first makes him truly a man.

~ Albert Schweitzer

Second Coming

He did indeed rise again in glory
to judge the living and the dead
Unseen by the religious and politicos of the day
His piercing light was eclipsed by the madness he found
So he left the sanctuary without a sound
befriending the trolls along the bridges
Walking hand in hand with the angels unaware –
the truly weak and sickly pilgrims

Our Lord, he came again and disappeared
into the crowd
becoming one of them
Passing through the marketplace
invisible and obscure, lost in the nape of the favelas

Shrouded in the clothes of the familiar
hiding in the moans
and screams of death and poverty
A leper and martyr among the boxes and alleys
meshing his greatness with the urban crazies

A forgotten savior holding court
among the homeless
crippled and reeking of despair

Waiting for open hands and smiles
For someone to mix their spittle with the clay
To give sight to the blind – to rub hope into their day

For someone, somewhere to pass their healing hands
over the crooked and the lame
To guide the rusted chariots to the Promised Land
beyond the lies of the political prophet's song

Hoping to find the faithful and lost among the crowd
Waiting for one who would stoop to the ground
and write letters in the sand

To cloak the errant whores
while others cast the first stone
hoping to find the faithful and lost among the crowd

Beseeching the poor in spirit, the blessed ones
the children of the ever-after
to rise up and give flowing cups of cold water

Lions

I am over the jet lag, but my mind is still on Kenya –
Somalia –
Rwanda –

Like a newsreel flashing in an old-time theatre
The trip keeps replaying in my mind.

May 10, 1994
Nelson Mandela Inaugurated
President of South Africa

I saw a lion on safari. It took us two hours and many elephant and wildebeest sightings to find him. The driver said it is good luck. Panthera Leo of the Serengeti. Perched in an acacia, golden halo gracing his head.

The Akagera runs red with the blood of Tutsi. Bodies floating on Lake Victoria. NGOs all flee Rwanda. Terrified, making their escape.

Somali warlords meet in Nairobi at a four-star hotel, cradled in the lap of luxury. They relish their power, eating meats and desserts while the Somali people starve to death in their war-torn country. Refugees amass on the Somali-Kenya boarder. Daily shipments of miraa are loaded onto cargo planes at Wilson Airport, headed for Mogadishu.

May 16 1994
Time *magazine cover: "'There are no devils left in hell,' the missionary said. 'They are all in Rwanda.'"*

Cynicism and apathy in the West.

America still reeling from the soldiers being dragged through the streets of Mogadishu.

May 19, 1994
Jackie Onassis Dies

Where is the compassion and civility?
It is the end of Camelot;
there are no Knights.

Every day there are more reports of people killed in Rwanda.
Something terrible is happening –
You can feel the tension in the air.

June 17, 1994
Game 5 of the NBA Playoffs
Rockets and Knicks

Don't really want to be here. Not a big basketball fan.
Tomato bruschetta and a bottle of red –
my contribution to this little party.

Men in the living room. Beer, chips, wings.
Television blaring.
"Ewing scores!"
Their yells escalate like growls
from lions on the Serengeti,
roaring over the announcer.
Pacing and anxious. Hunting prey –
male ESPN behavior.

Girls in the kitchen. Eating bruschetta,
drinking wine out of mason jars.

We are all in our forties, some closer to fifty. Three couples.
Darla and Lonnie are hosting. They met in the seventies.
Do-gooders who once wanted to save the world.
Their house smells of patchouli.
They have left their Birkenstocks
and all that save-the-world-stuff behind.
Total corporate animals now,
in debt like every other American.

From the living room –
lions roar for more chips and beer

After a few too many glasses of red
my somber mood is fading from the buzz.
Africa's plight is not as troubling the more I drink.
We are all talking loud. Girl talk. Gossip. Laughter.
Pizza is delivered.

The lions become enraged, roaring loudly,
Their growls escalate.

"Oh, you guys, don't get so upset; it's only a
game!" Darla yells. "Maybe if we still smoked weed the guys
would mellow out!"

"Damn, what is this crap? What about the game?" Lonnie roars
at the television. "O.J. Simpson, what the hell?"

The other lions join in, growling,
pacing, prowl –
restless in front of the television.

We refill the mason jars and take pizzas into the living room.
Hovering around the big screen.

Channel surfing to no avail. The game is interrupted by the
LAPD chasing O.J. Simpson in his runaway Ford Bronco.

"It looks like O.J. is getting his last fifteen minutes of fame,
huh?" Darla laughs. "That's okay, guys, he's almost home,
and then this O.J. thing will be over and we can get back to
what's important."

Skirt

A silent scream fills the pockets of
the equatorial corridor of East Africa

the folds of her crimson-and-amber scarf
swaddle tightly poverty and hunger

weaving sadness in the endless beauty
gifting treasures to the fertile soils

as the Akagera ripples scarlet
cascading down Rusimo
bestowing the sacred and forgotten into
the gracious cradle of Lake Victoria

She is humbled and broken
her hand reaching from graves and waters
wounded she is calling out

a maiden emptied of preciousness
her fabric unfurling

her skirt colorful and wide
pleated with sorrow

swallowing

the earth is cracking
swallowing the cries
of the hungry and poor

god's palm

the light through
branches pierce

cutting leaf
and blossom

gentle
and deliberate

like a graceful diamond

falling from god's palm

Lesa Caldarella-Wong

Regulars

Every morning I go to Starbucks
Seven a.m.
I am a regular
Venti Americano extra hot
With an extra shot, no room for cream
I sneak a Luna bar and banana
in my backpack with my laptop, and that is breakfast

People come and go during the ninety minutes
I sit and write, read the headlines
And people watch,
But mostly
People listen

I get the best perspective on world news
Hear the best stories
From the Regulars

A man
Called Smith
Late sixties
Faded Levis
Faded blue tee
Nikes
No socks
Ash white hair, steel-blue eyes

Strong and built
Leathered skin
Wrinkled with character
Got that way because of life

Too much sun, worked construction most his life
Until arthritis got the best of his back and knees
That and the 82nd Airborne
A few compacted discs, osteo, diabetes –
Side effects from Agent Orange
Pretty much every joint in his body is wracked with pain

That and his mind
Don't even talk about PTSD

He has stories
And I often wonder if they are true.

He talked a little about his first wife
His high school sweetheart
He was nineteen, she just turned eighteen
They married right before he left

She was already four months along
Right after the baby was born
She wrote him said she found
Another man, a good daddy, she said

He was devastated
Saw the baby twice
Too broken to fight
Signed the papers
He gave up his first child, a girl

Couldn't bear it
So he just disappeared
Keeps her photo in a box
With the flag and his medals

He just tuned out that pain
Jumping headlong into the mire
Did two tours

Saigon, Tet Offensive, Mekong Delta, and Cambodia –
Stories of love, stories of tragedy,
Stories of his buddies being blown apart
Left hanging in the trees –
In the middle of fucking nowhere,
In the middle of the humidity and deception

Of men too young and too naïve to be holding guns
Of napalm and burning flesh
Killing children and crawling through the mud –

Of missing the states
And everything that was familiar
Left to defend the world in a country
they didn't understand

He doesn't say much of those days
Except he misses the boys
He wonders about that woman he left in Saigon
Silky hair, silky skin, amber-brown eyes
The woman he loved
Sherri, he called her Sherri
Smith came back to the states after two tours
Married two times more

His second wife, Bonnie, was an ex
of his old buddy that died
He said she was a great cook, a good mom

They had two children
One daughter – a beauty, he says – perfect, smart
A son – died too soon at nineteen when his
alcohol-fueled night
Ended in a car crash – they never were close

Bonnie was a good gal,
But tired of his drinking, and his moods
His unexplained emotional distance
They divorced after thirteen years

His third wife
Smart, pretty
Funny
VA nurse
Had pity on him

He stopped drinking
Was going to the gym
Going to AA
Counseling and church
Going, going, going

But still had the demons in his skin
She could only handle his moodiness for three years
She said, "I deal with this shit every day, Smith. I love
you, but I can't do this. I am sorry, I can't do this."

The next day the closet was empty and she was gone.
She transferred out of state to another VA hospital.
That was eleven years ago.

He says,
Pity the women he married and tried to love

He was always on the outside of the dream
He lives alone now
Gave up the gym, AA, the church, and counseling

Loves his simple life
Walks his dog every day
Twice a month, he reads to the blind children
At the special school
He volunteers at the VA too
Just talking and listening – mostly listening to the
younger guys

Starbucks every morning
One of the Regulars
Black coffee
A piece of lemon pound cake
Reads the paper
He calls me Sherri
I laugh

A soldier's soldier
A man's man
The wise war hero
Tells me of his philosophy
He was beaten
He was broken and injured
Was medaled with the
Bronze and the purple
Was bought and sold

But he says
It is the service
And work of a solider
That gave him his will
Heard and smelled
Things you could never imagine
Was a doer
Still is

That is the only thing
That makes him
Feel
He is alive

That is his way
Of surviving
The pain

He is a soldier
And no matter what he does
Or who he becomes
He is
Always
Off to battle

Release

What is this fight?
This righteous and holy war?

Where the weapons of mass destruction?
The axis of evil – what is this valiant battle for?

As the blood runs in the streets
Blue to crimson
Where is the justice in this plot?
This battle has been going on for eons

Torn veils and broken bodies scattered on the land
New promises given and new deceptions born each day

With no regard for children's souls
Sacrificing babies
And mothers too

This conflict of spirit and wills
Rooted in centuries of power and hate

Sprouting
Like a thorny choking vine
Lush with vitriol
Void of blossoms and wine

While holy pilgrims pray each day
With a faith stronger than we could imagine

Cursing us and pleading with the same God
To save our souls and bless their warring actions

Never stopping to behold the sacred reflection
Of their brothers in the mirror

Never taking the deeper breaths of peace
Leading the path to their chosen land
And to their true release

Nest

Baby went away
Flying at his own request
Without regard
For the fair one's thought
He recklessly left the nest

Leaving broken promises and tears
Breaking the eggs of unbidden truth
Without thought for the crying
The pain he would cause
Lost in his madness and dark night

Leaving his lovers to weep
Dissolving rosary beads
Reciting over and over again –
Hail Mary, full of grace, the Lord is with thee;
blessed art thou amongst women …
Holy Mary, Mother of God, pray for us sinners,
now and at the hour of our death. Amen

Leaving his friends to ask why
To question the reasons and truth
Losing song in the bottom of empty beer mugs
And overflowing ashtrays

Selfish, indulgent refrain

Reaping harvests of guilt and regret
Fanning flames of melting candles
Combusting into unquenchable fires

Ruthlessly tearing the sacredness from
The Mother's Abode
He sleeps forever

Never grasping or knowing
That the power of a Mother's Love
Overshadows the migration of pain
For birds who leave the nest
The sacred thread
Holding the tapestry intact
Permeating the soul
Remains in her depths
For the son she bore

Cold Tile

Just a veil separates
Me
From the cold, cold tile

Just the mist of my prayers
Keeps the demons away

Peering through at me
With a smirking and hungry gaze

They sit on the tile
Barefoot, dirty
Lying in wait
For me to drop off to sleep

I can feel their hearts beating
And the pierce of their stare
Throwing darts at my face

I can see their thoughts in a cloud
Hovering above the bed
Violent, mocking, famished desire

Darkness fills the room

I lie peaceful
Feigning calm
Thinking of what
My next move will be

How can I make it seem
That I am not aware of this reality?

How can I look straight into
Their vacant eyes
Without fear
Knowing they have no souls

I will act as if I am beholding a king
I will smile and give
Just enough of my shadow

And then I will close my eyes
And go within
Deep into my own heart and mind

I will find my own path to peace
I will hide my fear
Deep inside

They can never own or
Take my soul
I will be safe from their terror
And the dreaded dream of this cold, cold tile
I will not feel their touch

At the time when angels come
To take my hand
To lead me from this evil place

Away from the ugliness and stares
Away from the cold, cold tile

I will rend that veil
I will take hold of my voice
Whispering my strength into the wind
I will rise up and be whole again

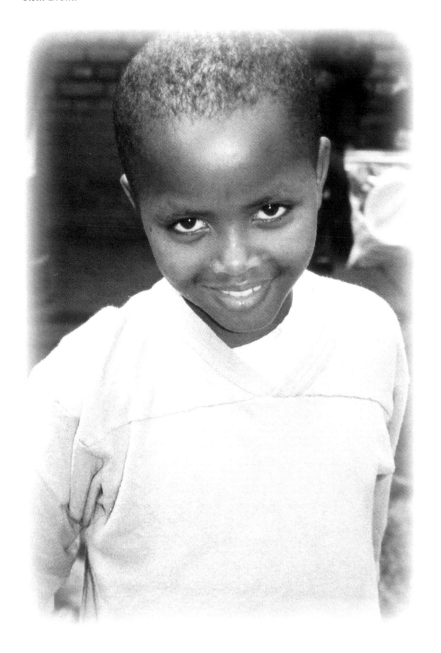

balm of Gilead

child soldiers
smiling
walking
arm-in-arm
a symbol of peace
children are the hope
keepers of the soul
balm of Gilead

Lie

No one to tell this story
No one to tell this lie

No one to keep this truth
Inside

No one to hide my smile
No one knows I'm here

No one to cry and scream
This metaphor of terror

No one, nowhere

To know this tree fell in the
Night

No one to know
The tears and fear
I hide

No one
Nowhere

To know this truth
To tell this lie

More than ever

Now more than ever it
is never enough
watching the weak
and the tough
fighting through life
and still ending up with
Nothing
To show for the
moments spent
Waiting and wanting more
than life was willing to give
or they were willing to accept
and live with
The battle of ways and wills
intersecting –
misdirecting of energy
Perfecting the –
extremes of what
should be
Pushing and pulling
the synergy of what could
save their
sacredness

Once again praying
and lighting incense for
those that are aghast at what
will come to pass
Seems like it is never
enough
And now more than ever
one
small victory
To overcome all the disappointment
and tragedy
would be especially
good
particularly sweet
Now more than ever just one
Brass ring
one good fortune
one lucky star
Just one, just
one
for the downtrodden
and weak

Would restore the
belief
and build faith in
mankind
And now more than ever
that answer to prayer
that conversation with
God
Would be just the right light
to lead the way there
to that
moment
in time
Where now
more than ever
we count the
rosaries of our life

sending regrets

the water's kiss
at river's edge
lapping hungrily
losing thoughts and affection

gazing at window and mirror
becoming memory
amongst the mud and moss

blurring reflection

tossing regrets
out like rings
from the verse and rhyme
bracing tide

traveling to islands
in nape of the rush
beyond the horizons
and bosom of the current's sleep

out of mind and sight
the messenger's stolid crush

lamenting pause and waves
waiting for the pleasures deep

traversing blue and gold
with blossom in the hull

settling calm and serene

sending what remains
across to the other shore

Possessed

Creating life without regard for what is holy
Eating their own offspring
Violating the innocence of angels

What possess these creatures
who once suckled their own mother's breast
to embrace such perversion and evil?

How could those who came into existence the same as lambs
and kings so easily subjugate and defile their own children
and heirs?

Tearing joy from the petals of flowers,
forever altering the sunset and sparkle of the stars.

Evil kings destroying the spirit
and shadows of the seraph so fair.

Causing madness and rage to fester in the shadows.

Courting hell and capturing the hearts and souls
without regard for the suffering they cause.

No greater sadness or shame exists.

Surrender

I will paint this canvas with the moments that do not yet exist
the warm and hallowed nape of trees

the stillness of the pond after the storm has left
the reflection of sorrow
and the sting of perfection's ample yoke

the disappointment and sadness-wrapped days
dressed in the clothes of the familiar

the reticence of dawn blending in with the music lovers make
the songs of childless mothers and grieving widows

I will embrace the sadness before the compromise
accepting the smiles and nods of strangers on my journey
surrendering to the graces golden and the tumble of my flaw

Sweeping the richness of the dawn
upon the red rock and gale within tears

catching the voice beneath the blossoms
not yet fully open with radiant centers and saffron stamen

And for that second before
and just upon the crest of dawn
see a glimpse of what the children of the morning will become
not yet conscious of the god within their pockets

innocent and unaware of the depth of their fate
this moment is forever emblazoned upon hearts

As we mourn the dreams they never dreamt
the tomorrows they never tasted
the happiness not yet relished

Standing on the edge
we will bid voyage to the beloved as they leave this abode
cast safely in the memories of their charges

mirroring guilt and resolve
they brace the passage sacred

Some suffer with blood turning to dust
within the balance of uncracked eggs and righteousness
Some cede their souls to the ether
consumed by all they have become
cradled by the remains of their shadows

But the children of the morning
are wrapped around our spirit –
we are beyond emotion

Their laughter triumphs and their candle remains
shining like a moment of universal love and sadness
our forever angels and eternal flame

IV
Pale Dogs

*There are people in the world so hungry that God
cannot appear to them except in the form of bread.*
~ Mohandas K. Gandhi

pale dogs

in the marketplace among the pale dogs
the children poor and free
with hunger in their swollen bellies
run barefoot on the hardened clay

greeting the day without care
weaving their laughter into song
while their tummies rumble music

indeed to spite the lack of sup – they are complete
their lives couldn't be fuller

teaching of real bread
as angels unaware

looking to the hills and sky
surveying the kingdom at their feet

their sweetness runs like rivers
beside the pale dogs

Baggage

In Beira
There are two of us

Sitting in the small terminal
Staring out the window

I'm waiting to hitch a plane ride
Headed for Maputo

We are strangers
He is reserved, preoccupied
I am sure he is a Brit

A pilot signals to him
From the tarmac
Through the window

There is one seat available

Leaving the terminal
Walking away

He turns
Looking at me

No words
He nods and smiles
Like a familiar friend

Holding a small steel suitcase
He boards the plane

One week later
Bahir Dar

After two body searches
Opening and closing suitcases
Checking and stamping passports
Three times

Security directs passengers
To line up and identify our baggage

On the tarmac
The plane is waiting

Debris and carcasses of burnt planes
In the tall grass next to the runway

Eighteen people
Confusion

Duffels
Samsonites
Huge straw bags
Backpacks

A large tweed suitcase
With fraying corners and broken latches
Bursting open
Held shut with a belt

Checking passports for the fourth time
They count passengers and baggage

We line up to board the plane to Addis

I have my large dirty duffle in hand
My camera bag and pack on my shoulder

I see him, the Brit
Joining the line

Holding his small steel suitcase

He nods
Reaching his hand out
Offering to carry my duffle

There are no words
He carries my bag up the stairs
Into the plane

He smiles
Like we have made
Love a thousand times

better woman

sitting here cup in hand
fingers banding around
my hot mug
barely sipping
my too-creamed coffee

in the clothes of the familiar
without my face
possessing only soul
and just a trace
of my beauty

with my rosary beads
saying prayers
in my sacred space

asking saints and angels
for that eternal balance
and rhythm for my song

knowing all along
that this silent sitting
is all the meditation
this catholic girl can muster

as I leave this inner sanctum
I will take with me
heart and purpose
bracing the inside
track of the miracle

and move into that place
of nowhere
that life of void
and measure

and return again
sipping too-creamed coffee

sitting in the clothes of the familiar
without face
and a better woman

Requiem

Sum and fragment of this wine
Without fathers to harvest their souls
Soon-forgotten fruit
Tumbling sweetly without rhyme
Floating through butterfly nets and floral arbor
No mothers to capture their dreams
Without cord or vine to bind them to the moment
The babies and precious ones bleed
Covered with steel-grey skies
And soiled cotton clouds
Too high and dense to catch
They lay open with tears and honey seeping
From the branches of trees
Offering sweet sacrifice
Screaming
Hosanna, hosanna
Lay the palm branches on our path
Lord of lords give us the sustenance of your vine
Give us resurrection and peace

holy place

with religious devotion
just after dawn
a faithful procession
of women gather

some have babies
tied to their backs
content and sleeping
unaware of the cadence
of hurried shoppers

fruits and vegetables
peppers, tamarinds, melons, cabbages
cassava, sweet potatoes, cocoyam
arranged
perfectly
like an altar
to honor the gods …

the women
entering
the holy place
causing riots as they
rummage through the displays

tossing and
squeezing the fruits
grabbing
the best of the bounty
pushing and shoving one another

overturning
the tables
of the temple
throwing jackfruit
assaulting melons
squashing
the preciousness
from the peel

without regard
for its sacredness
as if the flesh
will not break …
always pushing

near the trees

the water is ready for the tea

should we sit here under these
blossoms and leaves?

what is the story in these trees?

with their branches outstretched
will they tell us what they see?

we will sit and have tea
without a worry

only to be near to the trees
and closer to our truth

Wilson Airport
May 16, 1994

Migrating adventurers from the West
seeking holiday in treetops
and on safari

Hiking the broken escalator at Jomo Kenyatta
greeting the visa officials
with grins and loud "Jambos"

They cram the lobby of the InterContinental

Standing side by side
with weary NGO workers on their way
to the Kenya-Somalia border to give
food and medicines to refugees.

Gift-shop souvenirs
of kiondo bags
and colorful kanga fabrics
hanging like ripe fruit
and Christmas ornaments

The *Time* magazine cover headline: "There
are no devils left in hell," the missionary said.
"They are all in Rwanda."

Couples dressed in khaki
tote expensive cameras and backpacks
like tourist marsupials
Final destination – Maasai Mara.

Wary of matatus –
they ask the concierge to order
a London-style cab to Wilson Airport.

On the tarmac
a cargo plane under heavy police guard –
bunches of Kenyan miraa –
heading for Mogadishu

Somali men glistening in the sun
without smiles
Their teeth and tongues stained brownish-green –
their eyes a liquid sepia glaze

The Somalis and their pilot
chew miraa while they load
the precious cargo

The perfect panacea for hunger and poverty
Filling body
and mind with euphoria.

The flight to Maasai Mara is delayed.

The couples impatient –
pace the floors of the terminal.

Angry for the wait –
lost in their moment

Anxious to see the acacia trees
and wildebeest of the Serengeti

snowflakes

Jomo Kenyatta descent
aimless, inelegant albatross
breathlessly falling from the sky –

reckless
final approach
cast in the shadow
of the world's denial
the plane bounces on the runway

doubting its own commitment to land
amidst tragedy and
cracked eggs seeping
silent into the horizon

sojourners from the West
disembark

eager for repentance
offering bread and rosary
they weep for the missed moments

lighting candles
of penance – illuminating
sins of omission

their charity dots the acacia savannas
like giant snowflakes
resting unmelted
on the pinnacles of flowing blades of grass

their prayers in earnest and guilt
returning after the long rains
like a million birds greeting the fabric of the Serengeti –
a migration of recompense and shame

Maasai Mara

On holiday.
Maasai Mara.
Morning sun floods the plains.
Balmy wind –
tresses and worry blowing in the breeze.
Grasses dance to ancient music –
moving clouds across skies –
Moving wildebeest to the waters.

Acacia umbrellas like delicately woven lace parasols
covering Eden's paradise.

Thousands of birds, gazelles, and giraffe
humbly wander with symphonic purpose
postcard perfect.

Elephants larger than imagined
babies flawless
draped and wrinkled silver-grey replicas –
mothers stomping rumbles into the ground
creating maternal armor and refuge.

Panthera Leo, silken golden mane
gilded halo crown
illuminating regal stance.

Posed in acacia branch –
tail moving like a slow snake
deliberate, with ease.
Gracefully in rhythm with his breathing.

I can feel the absence of roar –
the shadow of his growl –
a king perched on the wall of the castle
standing over his subjects
his power and reign complete.

A mighty star with brilliant glow about to rise in the night.
Looking out over the savannah –
eyes like crystals cutting through the camera lens –
his consciousness all-pervading.

Magnificent animals emblazon the Serengeti like
flames.
following the north star of their survival –
full of danger and beauty –
never to be quenched or tamed –
Radiant creatures
spreading their fire across the plains.

Marketplace

it is Monday, seven a.m.
today I visit the marketplace
I am with the girl –
she does my laundry and cleans my house
knows the language, will do my bidding
she leads the way

makeshift shops lean
like old books on a shelf
bound by the dust
separate but together –
the bindings are worn
but the pages are still intact
each tells a different story

the merchant's tables –
colorful fabrics in piles
stacked high in pyramid fashion
baskets holding spices, coffee beans, and maize
nets hanging cradle bananas, limes

the throng of shoppers moves
in a chaotic and musical rush
clambering to get the best deal
pushing, pushing – always pushing
the pale dogs and barefoot children
weave through the crowd

happy, laughing
hungry and full of mischief

the aromas of cinnamon, cardamom, curry
tempt us with the yeasty goodness of
fresh-baked bread and samosas
mix with the dust wafting through the air
beckon us to the boulangerie

"we will come back for bread and cakes madame"
the girl leads me taking my hand
"Mondays and Wednesdays are the best days for meat
and fish"

walking through the ocean of madness
I follow her footsteps in search of meat and fish

straight ahead
one, no, two handsome men
standing out from the other shoppers and merchants
golden brown skin – exotic and graceful men
elegantly dressed – not part of the fray
they pass me in the crowd
almost brush my shoulder
I am tempted to reach out
so close I feel their shadows

I know that they each saw me
of course, how could they not?
I am a pale woman from the West

although I carry a basket –
I do not blend it
no matter how many nuances or customs I pick up –
I am not one of them

but still we could be lovers
or just friends –
we could share wine
have cheese and baguette –

they wander through the crowd
and disappear
sadness washing over me –
they are gone –

I follow the girl

the smell of ripe fruit
rising sweet in the morning
creates a wet warmth around us

stopping at the fruit stall
"madame, you want paw-paw?"

why is she asking me?

I have no time for this
I must find my lovers
where have they gone?
I know they must still be here
where did they go?

the girl is holding up
fruits and vegetables for my inspection
everyone is shouting
and holding up their fruits – pushing

she is fighting to get the best papaya
"not too soft, madame" she warns me
"this one, this one, this is perfect"

Peering through the
chaotic frenzy of fruit shoppers
I found them! I found my lovers!
I knew they would return –
I am certain I am being courted
yes I am sure they each gazed at me
for whatever remains of my beauty
I am happy to be indulged with their adoration
to be stared at and cherished
their eyes sparkling green glassine gems
cast in my direction
I look at them – pretending not to see
them drinking me in

Jarring me from my thoughts
the girl barks, "no, madame"
"take this bunch, this one has more"

"yes, this bunch is bigger," I agree
the girl pulls a leaf and puts it up to my nose
I smell something – basil and lemon

what are they doing?
they are walking away
they have scattered
my two lovers
each taking a different path

I stand on my tiptoes
pretending to look at the baskets – gazing

I only see one lover, just one
I wonder why my other lover left me
but one lover, can't that be enough for me?
yes I will manage with one lover…

he is looking my way
laughing, smiling
I feel my face get red
knowing I am being admired

I hold my wrap up to my cheek –
I am coy, I am mysterious

can he tell I do not speak a word of his language?
I can ask for coffee and basics
I know nothing of proper language
but then do lovers really need to speak?
can't we just love?
we can make our own language

I will spoil him
make him a sumptuous meal
bring him tea
be the best lover and friend
listen intently to his stories
be the best courtesan
the shameless concubine
posing with my best profile
my curve and blush intact
without words, with full intention

the girl is pulling me through the crowd
toward the meat and fish

another crowded stall
women with already-full baskets
shouting and pointing
the meats hanging in the sunlight
some glistening sweet with fat
leathery and covered with flies

damn! there is never cheese here
how I love cheese
and wine, a good glass of red, yes
my lover prefers red
and fresh baguette with cheese
truly a lovers' feast
and music, yes there must be music

chickens unaware of their fate
dance in their pen
make low clucking chirps
barely heard through the noise of the crowd

watching my lover as he shops –
what is that I see?
he is selecting flowers
he is gathering a bouquet for me
a sweet seduction
I must hurry the girl
I must tell my lover of the plans
he will visit, he will bring flowers

the girl is looking at the meats
"madame, yes, it is good meat, fresh today – it is good"
she selects some lamb and goat
she argues and gets a good price
I am happy she is doing the bidding
I smile like a polite pale woman

I smell fish
hanging like a canopy
trapped in heat of day

the merchant holds up a large fish
she shakes her head in disapproval.
"no, no madame – not good, not today …"

we return to the boulangerie
intoxicating smells – samosas, brioche, almond cakes

the taste, the desire of cheese and wine
taunting, seducing
sipping from the glass of my lover
breaking bread, the communion of saints
sharing it with a graceful and golden man
drinking the edges of his kisses
eating the fruit around the core
the grapes one by one …
"madame," she taps my shoulder
"the bread looks fresh – it will be good with the meat, yes?"
"and cake too – for tea" she adds
again I nod in agreement

I will prepare for the moment
I will boil water in the outside kitchen
adding buckets to the tub - making a bath.
floating herbs and petals in the water
making myself beautiful for my lover

splashing the warm water over my shoulders –
shoulders he loves to kiss.

he will join me at the bath
loosen my hair combs
my hair will tumble down
kneeling he will fill the pitcher with warm water
pouring it through my hair

the girl argues with the baker and asks to
squeeze every loaf …
I smile politely
looking down – embarrassed to make eye contact
happy to have someone to do my bidding
satisfied, the girl selects baguette, samosa, and almond cake

I will pick the petals and herbs on the walk back.
there will be no cheese, no wine. but we will love
he will bring flowers
such a considerate lover
there will be music, passion

juggling my baskets of breads and fruits
excited to be leaving the marketplace
I look up
desperate search among the sea of faces
where has he gone?
I have lost my lover in the crowd
tears flood my face

holding my passion within
longing for wine, cheese
for music
for that hot bath with herbs and petals

knowing this moment will never come again
taking leave with my parcels

I will buy fish on Wednesday –
That is the best day

common fish

my lord he came and went beneath the sea
without cloak or crown
into the deepest oceans of humanity
unbeknownst to kings and diplomats
dressed in the visage of the familiar
walking among the common fish, the pale dogs

my lord he rode upon the waves
to the sad and nameless places
breathing in the souls and faces
of the strangers and the crazies

swimming silent and effortless
beyond the eloquence and repartee
of self-proclaimed politicos and thieves

diving over the prophet's bridges
drinking and hiding the theologian's tea
taking sup from paper bags and paupers' cups
imparting honor and reverence
as he watched the queens and old men sleep

my lord he wept alone without a poet's song
knowing that his tears belong to the misbegotten soldiers
and the weight of lover's sorrow rests upon his humble shoulders

blessings to the wise he will surely send
when the wind does bend the sand
then my lord will make his altar
for the true upon this land

waiting for the moon to saunter
for the tides and river's passion to flow
exposing shells and Neptune's gems
for the folk to claim their souls

casting truth upon the air
radiant and beautiful
knowing what the urchins wish
and their hearts behold

then our lord will seek the shore
he'll take the hands of common fish
and kiss the brow of pale dogs
guiding us to heaven's door...

The problems we face today—violent conflicts,
destruction of nature, poverty, hunger and so on—
are human-created problems which can be resolved
through human effort, understanding, and the
development of a sense of brotherhood and sisterhood.
We need to cultivate a universal responsibility
for one another and the planet we share.
~ The Fourteenth Dalai Lama

Reflections from the Author

In 1994, I traveled to Africa on two separate occasions during one of the most tumultuous times in the history of that continent. My usual assignment was stateside in marketing and communications, working with volunteers and churches to raise funds and awareness for humanitarian causes. The purpose of my travel was to gain insight into the needs of the people we served, to visit projects currently sponsored by the organization, and to deliver supplies to children who had survived the massacre in Rwanda.

In that capacity, I was able to witness firsthand the impact and tragedy of poverty, war, famine, landmines, and the awful genocide in Rwanda, as well as rejoice in the election and inauguration of Nelson Mandela as South Africa's first black president.

The genocide in Rwanda was unique as the most horrific systematic murder of people in a 100-day span as the world stood by, watching without action and turning a blind eye to the holocaust.

I am humbled and grateful for the transformative and sobering lessons of that journey. And although the poetry in this volume is not strictly autobiographical, it is inspired and informed by my experiences and, in some cases, directly reflective of my trip notes and journals.

My experiences in Africa have shaped my worldview over the last twenty years. I am forever mindful of mankind's responsibility to look beyond their own world and to live lives of compassion and awareness.

LCW
Sacramento, California
January 6, 2014

*The idea that some lives matter less is the root
of all that is wrong with the world.*

~ Paul Farmer

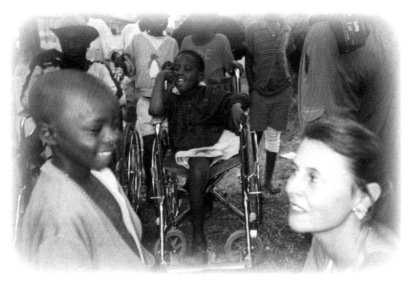

About the Author

A Southern California native, Lesa Caldarella-Wong spent more than thirty years working for non-profit organizations. She has a passion for people and the issues of social injustice, war, hunger, natural disasters, and human rights.

In her work for non-profit organizations, she has traveled throughout the world and facilitated national and international campaigns to aid victims and refugees of the 1994 Northridge earthquake, the Rwandan genocide, 1998's Hurricane Mitch, and the 2004 Indian Ocean earthquake and tsunami.

Having grown up in an Italian-Irish family of six girls, her writing is greatly influenced by her upbringing, her work with nonprofit organizations, and her first-hand experiences in third world countries.

She lives in Northern California with her husband and has three adult children, including an adopted son from Vietnam. *Real Bread* is her first book.

Photo and Design Credits

Cover, book design and typesetting by Ron Birchenough, Inkwell Productions

Front cover photo Dennis Albert Richardson/ Shutterstock.com

Back cover photo of author in Ethiopia, photographer unknown, author owns photo rights

Page 31,Hector Conesa/Shutterstock.com

Page 33, Matej Hudovernik/Shutterstock.com

Page 57, Bruce Raynor /Shutterstock.com

Page 81, Matt Berger/Shutterstock.com

Page 93, Wardon Wong

Page 141, Arend van der Walt/Shutterstock.com

Page 145, Elizabeth and Claighton Byrn

Page 157, Bruce Raynor /Shutterstock.com

Pages, 162-170, author in Ethiopian and Rwanda, photographer unknown, author owns photo rights

Portrait of author, page 168, Wardon Wong

All remaining photos in the in the book are credited to Lesa Caldarella-Wong